# TROMPE L'OEIL
## USING
# STENCILS

*A step-by-step guide to creating*
*three-dimensional effects for the home*

## LYNDA MILLS

SEARCH PRESS

First published in Great Britain 1999

Search Press Limited
Wellwood, North Farm Road,
Tunbridge Wells, Kent TN2 3DR

ISBN 0 85532 871 1

**Suppliers**
If you have difficulty in obtaining any of the materials and
equipment mentioned in this book, then please write to
the Publishers, at the address above, for a current list of
stockists, including firms who operate a mail-order service.

For more information about trompe l'oeil stencilling or for
details about any of the designs featured in this book,
please contact the author at: 37 Whitelands, Fakenham,
Norfolk NR21 8EW   Tel: 01328 856363

**Publisher's note**
All the step-by-step photographs in this book feature
the author, Lynda Mills, demonstrating how to
create trompe l'oeil effects with stencils. No models
have been used.

Colour separation by P&W Graphics, Singapore
Printed in Spain by Elkar S. Coop. Bilbao 48012

*This book is dedicated to my terrific family:
Dave, my ever-supportive and encouraging
husband, and our children, Jonathan,
Corinne and Christopher – our challenge
and delight!*

*My thanks to my friend of many years,
Dee Keller, who shared her love of
stencilling in those early days, along with
her heart.*

# Contents

# Introduction

Welcome to the fascinating world of trompe l'oeil stencilling!

*Trompe l'oeil* is a French term which literally means 'deceiving the eye'. It is now a term widely used to describe any decorative art which imitates reality. In stencilling, this is usually accomplished by creating shape, volume, texture, shade and shadow.

Over the centuries, the art of stencilling has been revered and respected. Beautiful, fragile patterns have emerged from beneath layers of plaster and other wall coverings, each giving us valuable glimpses into the history of design. The stencil, in all its many forms, has long been the tool for producing repeated decoration, and much of our aesthetic heritage has been wonderfully recorded in paints and pigments.

Despite the constant thread of stencilled design weaving its way through history, the last few decades have seen a vibrant re-emergence and appreciation of the art. Stencilling is still simply the creative use of holes, yet it has broken through the traditional boundaries of simplistic patterns into sophisticated design. Advances in technology now mean that stencils can be precision-cut by lasers from fine, yet tough, flexible sheets – this allows pin-point accuracy for overlays and a greater potential for detail. New paint technology means that it is now possible to stencil on virtually any surface, and innovative techniques can be employed to create the illusion of reality.

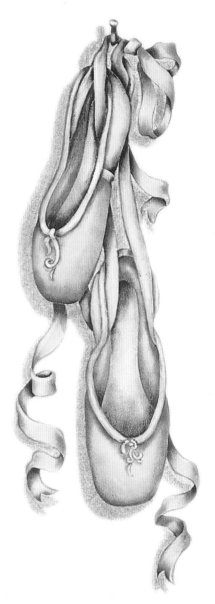

During the past decade and a half, my own stencilling style has developed. I have sought and tried many products, frustratingly made many mistakes, developed and abandoned techniques . . . but the resulting expertise has taken me all over the world teaching advanced stencilling skills, trompe l'oeil and muralling.

This book is designed as an unfurling revelation of stencilling techniques using progressive projects. As you turn the pages, you will begin your own journey. You may have stencilled before, but I have started at the beginning of the road. Together, I hope we will arrive at the place where you will feel inspired and empowered to attempt anything on the vast stencilling horizon.

Trompe l'oeil is great fun. It is delightful to see someone cross a room, intrigued by a shelf painted on the wall, and actually reach out and *touch* it in amazement. So, enjoy your creativity!

*Lynda*

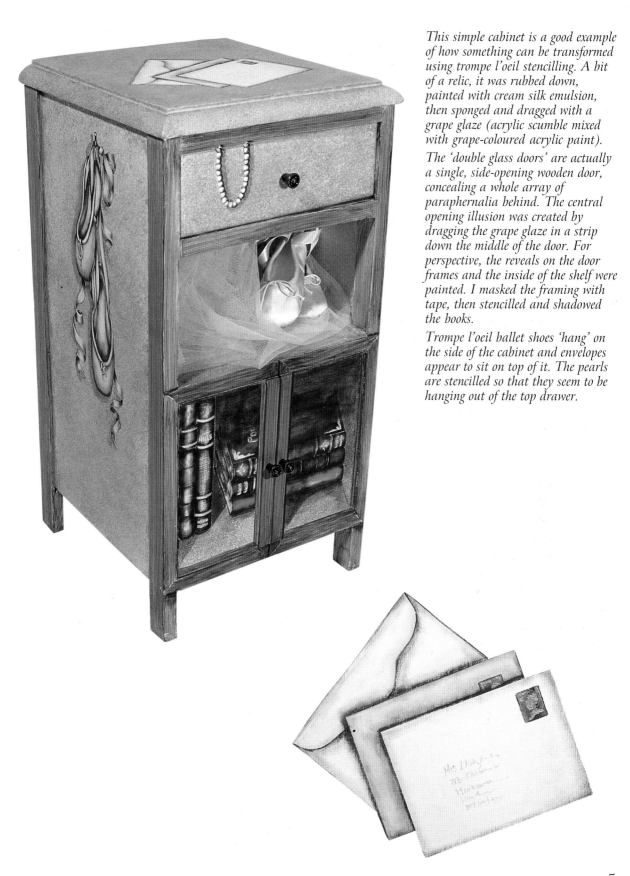

This simple cabinet is a good example of how something can be transformed using trompe l'oeil stencilling. A bit of a relic, it was rubbed down, painted with cream silk emulsion, then sponged and dragged with a grape glaze (acrylic scumble mixed with grape-coloured acrylic paint).

The 'double glass doors' are actually a single, side-opening wooden door, concealing a whole array of paraphernalia behind. The central opening illusion was created by dragging the grape glaze in a strip down the middle of the door. For perspective, the reveals on the door frames and the inside of the shelf were painted. I masked the framing with tape, then stencilled and shadowed the books.

Trompe l'oeil ballet shoes 'hang' on the side of the cabinet and envelopes appear to sit on top of it. The pearls are stencilled so that they seem to be hanging out of the top drawer.

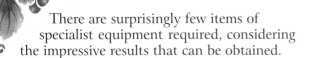

# Materials and equipment

There are surprisingly few items of specialist equipment required, considering the impressive results that can be obtained.

1. **Stencils** These come in various materials and cutting forms – at the most basic, you can hand-cut your own from card. Some stencils are supplied die-cut, but in my opinion, the best you can buy are laser-cut from mylar film. Precision cutting allows fine detail to enhance the design, and the accuracy essential when matching overlays. A good stencil is an investment, and distinctive design will create an impression that will be appreciated for years.

Stencils might just have a single sheet (or 'overlay'), but the most versatile are those with two or more sheets – these are called multi-overlay designs. Registration dots enable accurate positioning of each overlay in multi-overlay designs and precise placement when repeating borders. Usually, a small hole is cut into the corners of each sheet. You mark each hole as you stencil the first overlay, then carefully align all subsequent sheets, matching the dots.

Bridges are the narrow strips of stencil fabric that hold the design together and allow the background colour to show through when painted. The grapes above left are stencilled in the traditional method using a bridged stencil. The grapes above right are an example of bridgeless stencilling.

2. **Scrap paper** for practising colours, techniques and for preparing overlay prints. Wallpaper lining paper is ideal.

3. **Glass cutting mat** for cutting your own stencils. Self-healing cutting mats tend to restrict the free movement necessary for cutting with a scalpel, and are inappropriate for use with a heat pen.

4. **Ruler** for cutting straight lines and checking measurements.

5. **Scissors** for cutting masks.

6. **Heat pen** for cutting stencils and making registration dots. A single hole punch can also be used for registration. Cutting stencils by heat pen tends to create less accurate edges, but can be faster than a scalpel, and useful when cutting rough edges.

7. **Permanent pen** for tracing a design when making your own stencils or masks. It is also used to identify registration dots on the first overlay.

8. **Scalpel** for cutting out stencils. A heat pen can also be used.

9. **Paper towel** can be used to dab your brushes on and so avoid excess paint reaching your work – this is essential when using the dry-brush technique. I tape a sheet on to my palette. Paper towel can also be used to mop up any spills, or it can be dampened and used to prevent brushes drying out.

10. **Cotton buds** for cleaning up any smudged edges or making other small corrections.

11. **Drafting film** for making stencils and masks. Acetate can also be used to make masks.

12. **Shampoo** for cleaning brushes used with acrylic paint.

13. **Extender medium (retarder)** can be mixed with acrylic paint and used to prolong the workability of the paint. It will maintain the consistency while diluting the pigment. Shadowing is often painted with tinted extender. A little extender will also bring slightly dried-out brushes back to life.

14. **Invisible tape** for repairing damaged stencils.

15. **Spirit level** for ensuring work is horizontal or vertical.

16. **Low tack masking tape** for securing stencils in position and for marking registration dots. A low-tack tape will help to protect your paint surface. Spray adhesive is also available.

1. **Paints** There are many different types of paint available, but they fall into two categories: water-based and oil-based. All the paint used in this book for both background and decoration is water-based.

i. Water-based: Quality acrylics are by far the best for trompe l'oeil because of the intensity and opacity of the colour pigment. They are consistent in texture, and they are convenient and economical to use because you need so little paint. Acrylics come in a wide variety of colours and can be used on most surfaces, but you may need to add another product, i.e. fabric medium, to ensure stability. You can work with quite a small selection of colours, and mix and blend your own from these. Brushes can be washed immediately after use in warm water and shampoo.

ii. Oil-based: Specialist stencil crayons and creams are available on the market, and these can produce a lovely soft finish. However, they take time to dry, and are not really intense or opaque enough for effective trompe l'oeil.

2. **Brushes** Brushes are really important to the trompe l'oeil stenciller. For most stencilling, select soft bristles with well-flagged ends (hairs split at the tips). More resilient bristles will give a good stippled effect, which is particularly useful where texture is needed (i.e. for brickwork or fur), but avoid any brush with an exaggerated blunt cut. It is best to use one stencil brush per colour to avoid muddying, and select brush sizes to suit the amount of coverage needed. Double-ended brushes are economical to use – a different colour each end halves the number of brushes you need to hold (and when you are high up, balancing on a scaffold, fewer brushes are a blessing!). Angled shaders are useful, especially when shadowing, and liner brushes are great for hand-finishing. You can stop brushes drying out by placing them on slightly dampened paper towel, and keeping them in a zip-up plastic bag during temporary breaks.

3. **Palette** Any non-porous surface is suitable. I use slabs of plastic, but you could use china or disposable plates, plastic film or glass. If you tape a piece of paper towel to your palette, you can dab your brush on to it before you work on your project, to prevent using the brush with too much paint on it.

Paint effect backgrounds will enhance your stencilling and trompe l'oeil. You will find the following materials useful:

1. **Vinyl silk or acrylic eggshell paint** is used for basecoating a surface.

2. **Scumble glaze** A water-based transparent glaze which is coloured with acrylics and brushed over a basecoat. The decorative paint effect is then worked on top.

3. **Water-based paint** provides the colour for mixing with scumble glaze.

4. **Woodgrainer** A rubber tool which can be dragged through glaze and rocked to produce an open woodgrain effect. There are also combs available which provide alternative patterns.

5. **Dragger** A brush with long bristles which creates the striped finish known as dragging.

6. **Softener brush** This is useful for softening many of the paint effects, such as colourwashing and woodgraining.

7. **Rag** For ragged finishes.

8. **Sponge** A natural sea sponge is used for sponging. Soak and squeeze before use.

# Using stencils

Borders ~ Corners ~ Freeform
Special features

Stencils come in many shapes and sizes. Do not
be daunted by the apparent complexity of a
stencil made up of several overlays – each
overlay is only a sheet of plastic with holes in it!

When selecting designs, consider the space
available and the overall effect you wish to
create. You have many choices, so allow yourself
to dream! Remember that stencils are your tool
to transform boring blandness into distinctive
design.

Stencilling has many practical advantages
over traditional wallpapers and pasted borders.
You are in control of colour, density of pattern,
and layout – you do not need to compromise.
Part of the design can be stencilled on to soft
furnishings such as curtains, cushions, throws or
tablecloths, as well as on to furniture and floors.
In this way, stencils can be used to coordinate an
entire room. All fashion is cyclical but stencilling
will accommodate and enhance all trends.

**ENGLISH ROSE BORDER**
*The English rose border shows a spaced
border. You could use another small motif,
such as a leaf to separate each cluster.*

**APPLE BORDER**
*This is an example of a
continuous border.*

## Borders

Borders are often what spring to mind when
stencils are mentioned. The fact that stencils are
repeatable means that they lend themselves
particularly well to producing borders, and they
are a very effective way of bringing designer style
to any room.

Customisation is a key to successful interior
design, and you can use a stencilled border to
accentuate or disguise a room's features. You can
add professional flourish by letting leaves
cascade down beside architrave, or you could
frame a feature, panel walls, divide space or draw
attention away from an area of architectural
weakness.

There are various forms of stencil borders.
The ivy (see page 12) is an example of a freeform
border, but the borders featured here show two
other types: the continuous and the spaced
border. The apple border runs continuously for
as long as you require. The English rose border is
a more flexible, self-contained design that can be
repeated immediately as shown here, or spaced
using, for example, a small leaf stencil.

# Special features

Stencilling does not just focus on borders or patterns – individual objects are increasingly popular. A stencilled hat 'hanging' on the back of a door would be intriguingly discreet (see page 14). Alternatively, a basket of flowers, a bottle of wine or a pair of ballet shoes might all be helpful in transforming a dull area into something special.

**TROMPE L'OEIL CUPBOARD**
*Trompe l'oeil books decorate this cupboard door. The same stencil is used for both the upright and horizontal books. Real handles add the final touch and help convince the eye that the one solid wooden door is really two glass doors.*

**MAGNOLIA HAT**

*This trompe l'oeil magnolia hat is stencilled on to a rag-rolled background. Despite the strength of the lilac paint effect, the hat still stands out because of the effective use of shadowing.*

# Paint effects

Rag-rolling ~ Sponging on ~ Colourwashing
Woodgraining ~ Dragging

In recent years, paint effects have become increasingly popular as an alternative to a flat paint finish. They are easy to do, and are amazingly effective.

To create a rich background to complement your stencilling, you should begin by painting your surface with a basecoat of vinyl silk or acrylic eggshell, then allowing it to dry.

The recommended glaze for all paint effects is an acrylic scumble. I mix this with an artist's acrylic paint to the colour of my choice. Quality artist's acrylic is strong in pigment, so when mixing scumble glaze you will need approximately 20 parts scumble to 1 part paint. If using emulsion paint, you can use much less scumble – 1:6 is fine. You can also make a glaze by diluting emulsion paint with water. However, this mixture will dry fast, and will probably not allow you time to finish the effect evenly or disguise the joins – the result could therefore be patchy. It is a good idea to wear protective gloves as glazes can be quite messy.

## Rag-rolling

This produces a plush finish, similar to crushed velvet.

Use clean, lint-free cloth. Tear the cloth into 45cm (18in) squares before you start. Soak one in water, then wring it out. As the square becomes saturated with glaze, rinse it in water, wring out and then retwist. When the cloth no longer gives a crisp pattern, change to another square.

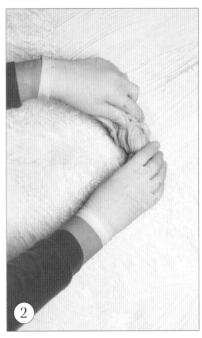

1. Load your brush with paint/ scumble glaze. Roughly brush the mixture on to your surface, using random strokes.

2. Fold and twist the cloth into a sausage shape. Roll it through the wet glaze, varying the direction, to create a pattern. Leave to dry.

# Sponging on

This is a very quick, easy and totally additive technique! I like to choose soft colours for this, to produce a really mellow effect.

It is best to use a natural sponge for this technique. Soak it in water and wring it out before use.

1. Dip a natural sponge into the paint/scumble glaze. Apply to your surface randomly, varying the direction to avoid a repeat pattern.

2. Repeat step 1 using a different shade of the same colour. Leave to dry.

# Colourwashing

This technique can be used to produce a beautiful soft and cloudy finish. The effect is subtly textured, with slightly uneven colouring, which suggests age.

1. Apply the paint/scumble glaze using random, cross-hatched brushstrokes.

2. Dust over the surface with a softener brush to remove harsh lines. Leave to dry.

# Woodgraining

This technique is surprisingly simple yet stunningly effective. Woodgraining is used mostly on furniture or doors, as it can be quite difficult to keep the pattern even over a larger area.

I find it useful to have a rag or paper towel to hand to clean excess paint off the tool at the end of each stroke.

1. Apply the paint/scumble glaze in a downward motion, using fairly even strokes.

2. Pull a woodgrainer down through the paint, rocking it gently as you go. Try to get the knots in different places in each adjacent line. Leave to dry.

# Dragging

This is another simple and subtle technique. It is best used in small areas as breaks in a long stroke are usually obvious.

Use enough pressure to allow the bristles of the dragger brush to splay slightly. At the end of each stroke, scissor-clean the dragger by pulling it between fore and middle fingers. You can return the excess glaze back into its container and use it for subsequent strokes.

1. Apply the paint/scumble glaze in a downward motion, using fairly even strokes.

2. Pull a dragger brush down through the glaze with enough even pressure to create strong lines. Leave to dry.

# Creating form

Shaping curve ~ Using colour shading

Creating form – or shaping – is the first important skill that a good stenciller needs. Shading for curve is the technique used to define shape and form. If an object is painted with a single tone of a colour, it will appear flat. Shading with colour will instantly create shape. My simple rule is: lighten the areas nearest you and darken those further away.

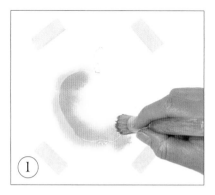

① 

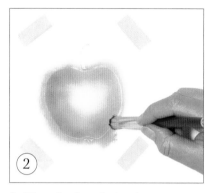

②

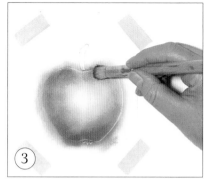

③

1. Use the stencil brush in a swirling motion to apply a green basecoat. Begin at the edges, and gradually work in towards the middle. Do not colour the centre itself if you are working on a light background.

2. Use the brush in the same swirling motion to apply a darker shade of green around the edge.

3. Swirl in red to one side of the apple.

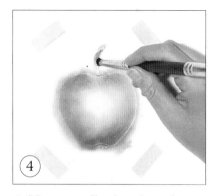

④

⑤

4. Use a smaller brush and brown paint to add the stem and the calyx. Work in short sweeping movements.

5. Add black to the base of the stem and lower edges of the apple to suggest weight and form.

18

### BUD

*This is a good example of how a simple object is made up of a series of curves. Notice how just a few sweeps of the stencil brush convey the impression of shape.*

### VASE

*Curves shape this vase. Notice too how, in trompe l'oeil, the shade used for shaping also combines with shadows.*

### BASKETWORK

*Basketwork is a favourite of mine. Notice how this detail shows the undulation of the weave, which comprises a complex set of curves.*

# Rose border

Using a bridged single overlay stencil ~ Cutting a stencil
Dry brush technique ~ Swirling ~ Stencilling leaves

This book is intended to inspire, but it is also designed to
progressively build skills and confidence. Each of the projects
which follow, includes the pattern for you to produce your own
stencils. You can enlarge them to size on a photocopier and trace
on to a good quality drafting film. Your stencil can then be cut
out.

   As the best place to start is at the beginning, this first project is
a simple, bridged, single overlay border design. I show you how to
cut the stencil, master the dry-brush technique, and begin shaping
curve with colour. It is a good idea to read through the project
before you begin, and then test colours and practise techniques on
scrap paper.

**ROSE LAMP AND
CUSHION**
*Stencilled designs
allow you to
coordinate fabrics,
furnishings and
furniture.*

**ROSE FRAME**

*This border design can be used as a frame to transform a rather bland wall into something sensational.*

## YOU WILL NEED

**Materials for stencil**: 1 sheet of drafting film, A4 (11¾ x 8¼in), permanent pen, masking tape, glass cutting mat, scalpel, heat pen or single hole punch

**Acrylic paint**: pink, burgundy, mid-green, dark green, gold

**Stencil brushes**: 3 x small, 1 x medium, 1 x large

**Other items**: palette, paper towel

**PATTERN FOR THE ROSE BORDER**

*Enlarge on a photocopier by 280% for a design 28cm (11in) wide.*

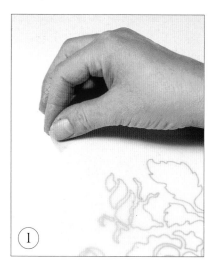

① 

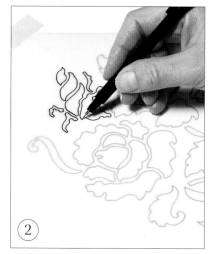

② 

③

1. Tape a piece of drafting film over the design.

2. Trace the outline of the design on to the film with a permanent pen.

3. Remove the pattern and place the film on a glass cutting mat. Do not tape down. Cut out the pattern using a scalpel, beginning with the smallest details. Mark the registration dots with a heat pen or single hole punch. Use masking tape to secure the stencil to your surface.

**NOTE**

To cut out a curve, hold the drafting film and move this, rather than moving the scalpel.

Any mistakes can be corrected by applying a piece of invisible tape to both sides of the stencil and recutting.

4. Decant small pools of each paint on to the palette.

5. Coat the bristles of a medium brush with pink paint. Dab the brush on to paper towel to remove excess paint.

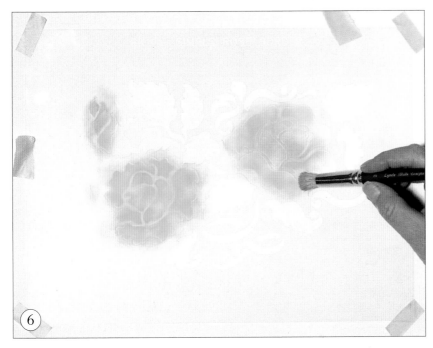

6. Work the almost-dry brush in a swirling motion to apply a basecoat of pink paint to the roses.

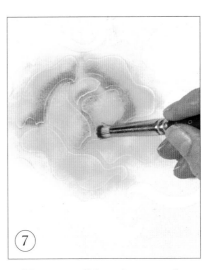

7. Use a small brush to scrub burgundy into the centre of each flower.

23

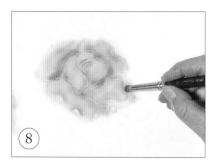

8. Swirl burgundy into the concave curves of the petals, to suggest curling edges.

9. Use a large brush to apply a mid-green basecoat to the leaves.

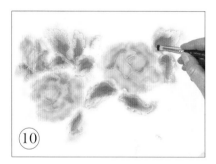

10. Use a small brush to apply dark green into the central vein of each leaf.

11. Use a small brush to apply burgundy over the dark green, and extend it further up the centre of the leaf.

12. Use the same brush to paint the ribbon burgundy.

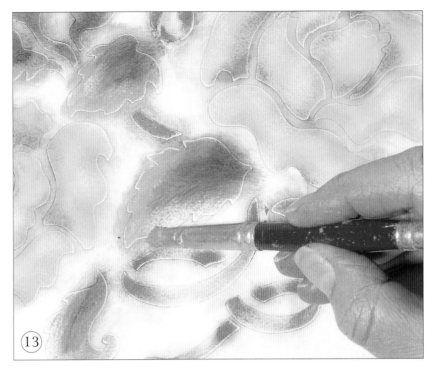

13. Use a small brush to stroke in gold from the edges of the leaves.

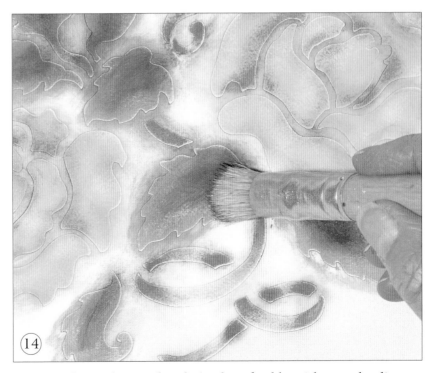

14. Use the mid-green brush (and preferably without reloading with paint) to blend the colours on each leaf to soften the effect.

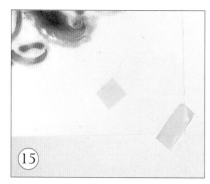

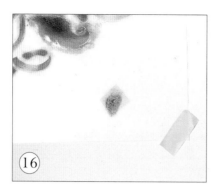

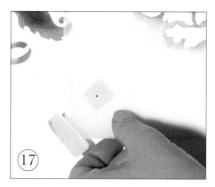

15. Remove the masking tape from one of the corners and place a small piece of tape underneath the registration dot. Secure the corner back in place with tape.

16. Using any colour, paint through the registration hole. Repeat the process for all registration dots.

17. Remove the stencil then reposition it to one side of the painted image to form the border. Match the registration dots and secure in place.

18. Repeat steps 1–17 to build up a border of roses.

**PINK ROSE BORDER**

*One of the many advantages of stencilling is that you have total freedom of colour and finish. This border was stencilled on to a sponged pink wall, in pastel shades.*

**GOLD ROSE BORDER**

*This is another variation, this time worked in gold on a terracotta colourwashed wall.*

medium, 2 x large, 1 x liner brush

**Other items:** palette, paper towel

○ *Overlay 1*

● *Overlay 2*

**PATTERN FOR THE TEDDY**

*Enlarge on a photocopier by 345% for a teddy 33cm (13in) tall.*

1. Tape a piece of drafting film on to the pattern and trace overlay 1 windows with a permanent pen. Label it *Teddy Overlay 1*.

2. Tape the second sheet of film on top of overlay 1 and trace round the overlay 2 windows. Label this *Teddy Overlay 2*.

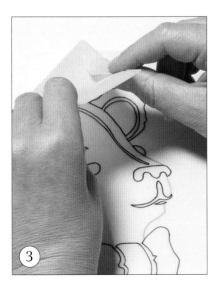

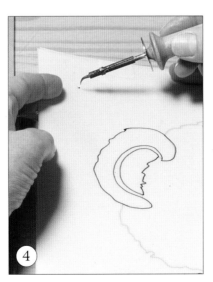

3. Carefully tape overlay 1 to overlay 2 and then remove them from the pattern.

4. Place the two overlays on a glass cutting mat. Use a heat pen or a single hole punch to mark the registration dots through both overlays.

5. Separate the two overlays, then cut out the windows (see page 22). Tape overlay 1 to your surface.

6. Load a large brush with dark brown on one side and light brown on the other.

7. Gently swirl the brush on the palette to mix the colours slightly. Dab the brush on to paper towel to create an almost-dry brush.

8. Mark the registration dots on small pieces of tape (see steps 15–16, page 26).

9. Roughly stipple all over the teddy's coat with the brown mixture.

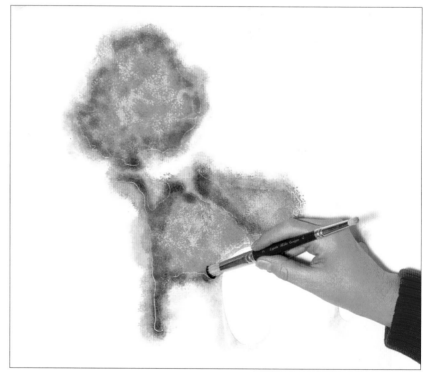

10. Use a medium brush and black to stipple around the edges of the windows to add shape and contrast to the teddy.

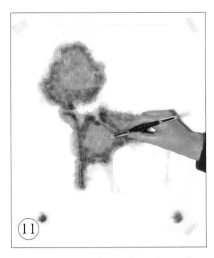

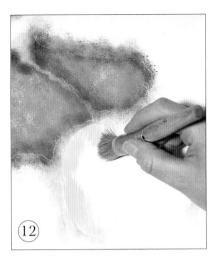

11. Use a medium brush and gold to add highlights to the centre of each shape.

12. Load a large brush with pale pink paint, then drag it down each paw.

13. Shade black around the edges of the paws with a medium brush.

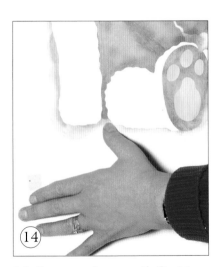

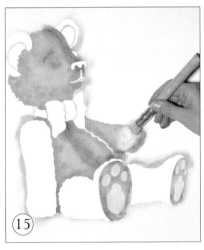

14. Remove the stencil. Position overlay 2 over the stencilled image. Match the registration dots exactly, then secure in place with masking tape.

15. Use a medium brush to apply white paint to the front paw pad.

16. Use the same techniques shown in steps 9–13 to stipple over the teddy. Do not colour the paws, the bow tie or the facial features. Add shape and contrast with black and use gold to add highlights.

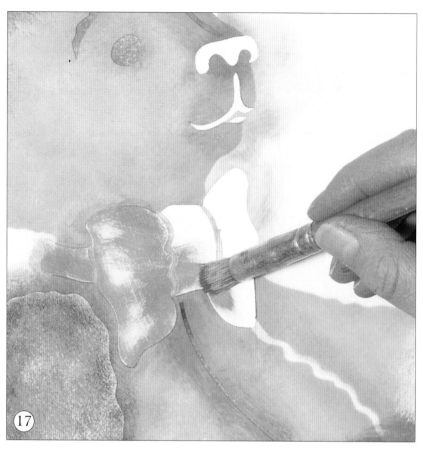

18. Use a small brush and black paint to add definition and shape to the bow-tie.

17. Load a medium brush with green. Drag the brush over the bow-tie.

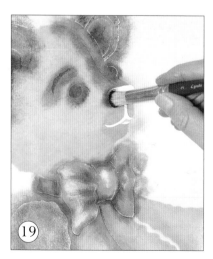

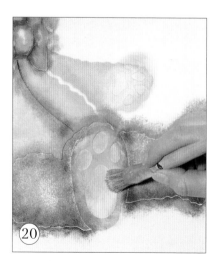

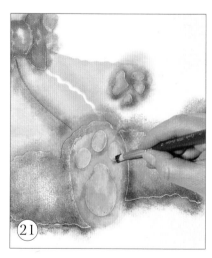

19. Use the same brush and black for the facial features and the line down the teddy's tummy.

20. Clean the brush used with pale pink on paper towel, then re-load with pink and drag each paw.

21. Use the small black stencil brush to stipple around the edges of the paw pads.

22. Use a liner brush to add a dot of white to each eye, and a stripe of white to the nose.

23. Remove the stencil. Make any colour adjustments you consider necessary.

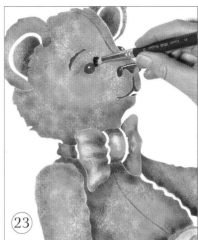

**THE FINISHED TEDDY**
*This endearing teddy will add a warm smile to any environment.*

# Grapevine

Using a bridgeless multi-overlay stencil
Subshading ~ Shaping

The next step in your progress is bridgeless stencilling. With no bridges to separate adjacent components as in traditional stencilling, you need to work a little harder defining shape and contrast.

The Grapevine stencil has three overlays, and is prepared in the same way as Teddy's overlays (see page 29).

This project also introduces subshading. This is a stencilling technique used to dramatically increase depth by contrast. By shading the edges of a feature that is behind another object you sink it back, therefore helping the front feature to 'pop up' when added or revealed later.

**Materials for stencil**: 3 sheets of drafting film, 43 x 33cm, (17 x 13in), permanent pen, masking tape, glass cutting mat, scalpel, heat pen or single hole punch

**Acrylic paint**: mid-green, dark green, burgundy, dark purple, light brown, dark brown, gold, black, white

**Brushes**: 5 x small, 3 x medium, 1 x large, 1 x liner brush

**Other items**: palette, paper towel

*Overlay 1*

*Overlay 2*

*Overlay 3*

**PATTERN FOR THE GRAPEVINE**
*Enlarge on a photocopier by 240% to create a design 38cm (15in) wide.*

**GRAPEVINE CHEST**

*This handsome pine chest was stencilled with the grapevine. The stencil was reversed to produce the image on the right. When the stencilling was complete, the entire chest was finished with antiquing wax.*

35

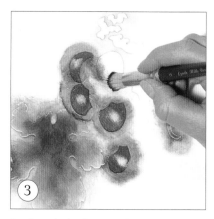

1. Use masking tape to secure overlay 1 in place. Basecoat the leaves and tendrils in mid-green, then work in dark green and burgundy (see pages 24–25).

2. Use a small brush and black to subshade the edges of the leaves next to the leaf tip turn.

3. Swirl dark purple paint around the edges of the grapes, leaving the centres untouched.

**NOTE**

**If working on a dark background, paint the centres of the grapes lighter using a mixture of white with a touch of purple.**

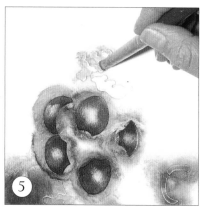

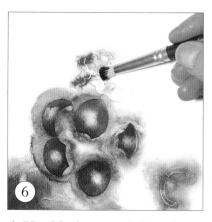

4. Use black and a small brush to subshade the edges of any grapes that will appear behind other grapes.

5. Stipple in the vine using a small stencil brush loaded with light brown.

6. Use black around the edges of the vine.

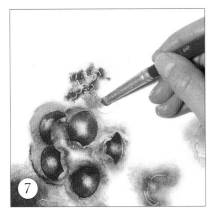

7. Use mid-green to paint the leaf tip that turns over.

8. Use gold to add highlights to the edges of the leaves. Work over the leaves in mid-green to soften the effect (see page 25).

9. Remove the first overlay then carefully position the second overlay on top of the image. Repeat steps 1–4 and 7–8 to paint in the leaves, tendrils and grapes.

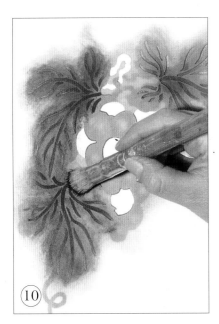

10. Remove the second overlay and position the third. Paint in the veins on the leaves using dark brown and a medium brush. Repeat steps 3–4 to paint in the grapes, steps 5–6 to paint in the vine, and step 1 to paint in the tendril.

11. Remove the third overlay. Add a highlight of white to the centre of each grape using a small liner brush. Check the overall colour balance and replace any of the overlays to re-stencil if necessary.

37

# Keys

Simple trompe l'oeil ~ Hand-finishing ~ Shadowing

This first trompe l'oeil project is designed so that you can continue to practise your shaping and subshading skills, but you should also learn how to introduce light and shadows to add to the realism.

   Before beginning any trompe l'oeil project, you should check the main light source in situ. Consider the direction and strength of the light and ensure all highlights, shade and shadowing are consistent throughout as you work. Prepare an overlay print and study the correlation of the design components. Mark the overlay print with any information regarding light, shade and contrast to help you as you work. Remember that as the keys are hanging vertically, their outline will be echoed on the wall as shadow.

**Materials for stencil**: 3 sheets of drafting film, 25 x 12.5cm (10 x 5in), fine permanent pen, masking tape, glass cutting mat, scalpel, heat pen or single hole punch

**Acrylic paint**: gold, brown, blue, black and white

**Stencil brushes**: 3 x small, 1 x medium, 1 x liner brush, 1 x small angled shader

**Other items**: palette, paper towel, extender medium

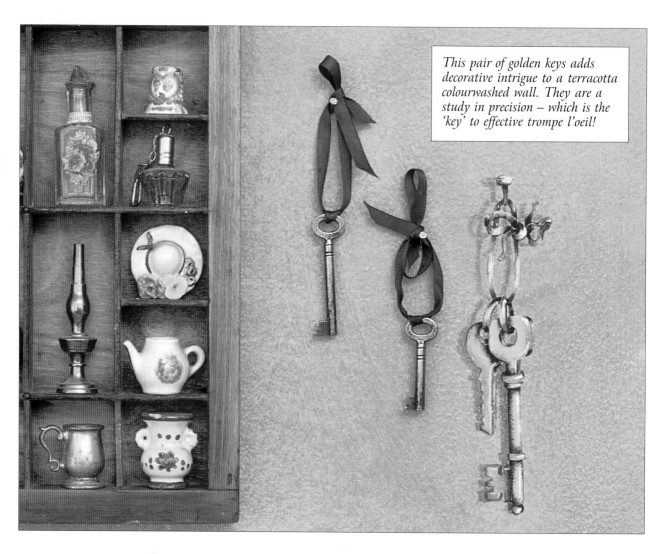

*This pair of golden keys adds decorative intrigue to a terracotta colourwashed wall. They are a study in precision – which is the 'key' to effective trompe l'oeil!*

**PATTERN FOR THE KEYS**

*Enlarge on a photocopier by 170% to get a design 18cm (7in) tall.*

- ⚪ Overlay 1
- 🔵 Overlay 2
- 🔵 Overlay 3

1. Tape overlay 1 on to your surface and mark registration dots. Use gold and a medium brush to basecoat the key and the nail head.

2. Use brown and a small brush to paint in the two shapes on the end of the key.

3. Use black and a small brush to shade the edge of the key barrel to suggest a curve. Use the same brush to heavily subshade the key to provide contrast.

4. Basecoat the ribbon using blue and a small brush.

5. Use black to add shape to the ribbon. Now remove the first overlay.

39

6. Position overlay 2 carefully, matching the registration dots. Use gold to basecoat the nail, the front of the ring, the horizontal band and the end of the key.

7. Use blue to go over the ribbon, and brown for the rest of the windows.

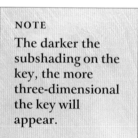

**NOTE**
**The darker the subshading on the key, the more three-dimensional the key will appear.**

8. Use black to add shading and shape to the key, the ribbon and the ring.

9. Remove overlay 2.

10. Position overlay 3, then basecoat the ribbon in blue and the keys in gold. Work the small sections at the end of the large key in brown.

11. Use black to add shading to the ring, the ribbon and to both keys.

**NOTE**
When painting shadows, remember to place them away from the natural light source in the room.

12. Remove overlay 3. Check for colour balance and contrast and re-stencil if necessary. Increase definition using a liner brush loaded with black paint.

13. Add white highlights to the nail and keys using the liner brush.

14. Add a few drops of dark or black paint to water or extender medium to dilute the colour. Use a liner brush or a small angled shader to paint in subtle shadows behind the keys.

# Shelf and crockery

Combining stencilled components
Creating woodgrain ~ Blanking out ~ Stacking
Eye level ~ Pitfalls to avoid

This next project has many lessons to teach. It introduces more textures, and explores the potential of a simple stencil packed with flexibility of use. The shelf is created with masking tape – so this can easily be adjusted to any length.

Stacking is the process by which depth is created, and it is achieved by placing objects behind or in front of others. Without this technique you would end up with a series of unconnected, isolated items that would look unrealistic. Stacking can be achieved in several ways – you can work forwards, i.e. blank out then overpaint the front feature, or work backwards ('stack-back'), i.e. place objects behind others. This illusion is created by masking, thus protecting the front object.

**YOU WILL NEED**

**Materials for stencil**: 2 sheets of drafting film 20cm (8in) square, and 1 sheet 12¾ x 9cm (5 x 3½in), 1 sheet of acetate 16 x 14cm (6 x 5½in), permanent pen, masking tape, glass cutting mat, scalpel, heat pen or single hole punch

**Acrylic paint**: brown, black, white, terracotta, yellow, green

**Stencil brushes**: 3 x small, 3 x large, 1 x liner brush and 1 x large angled shader

**Other items**: palette, paper towel, extender medium

**THE FINISHED SHELF**
*Trompe l'oeil stencilling can provide virtual reality for walls! Shadowing is simple to do and adds enormously to the overall effect of depth of field and light.*

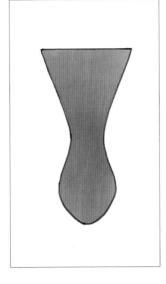

 *Overlay 1*

 *Overlay 2*

## PATTERNS FOR THE SHELF ITEMS AND SHELF BRACKET

*Enlarge on a photocopier by 200% to create a mug 12cm (4¾in) high and a bracket 7.5cm (3in) high. The main design is very versatile – it can be used to form a mug, milk jug, cream jug, coffee pot, sugar bowl and vase.*

## COFFEE POT

*A coffee pot is easy to stencil. Simply double the height of the mug's body, then add the knob, handle and spout. Remember to return to overlay 1 to print the neck of the knob after completing overlay 2.*

## VASE AND SUGAR BOWL

*Create a vase by masking out the handle, spout and knob on top, then extending the height of the basic stencil by repeating the body of the mug. By only stencilling half of the mug's body, you have a sugar bowl.*

## MILK AND CREAM JUGS

*You can add a spout to the mug stencil to make a milk jug. If you shorten the body you have a cream jug.*

1. Apply two lengths of masking tape to your surface, approximately 2cm (¾in) apart. Use a spirit level to ensure they are horizontal. These will create the front edge of the shelf. Place two short strips of tape down the sides.

2. Double-load a large brush with brown and black (see page 30). Drag the paint along the length of the shelf in long sweeping movements to create the impression of woodgrain. Lightly shade the edges with black using a small brush. Leave to dry.

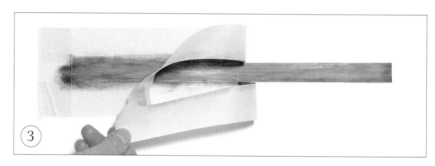

3. Remove the tape carefully.

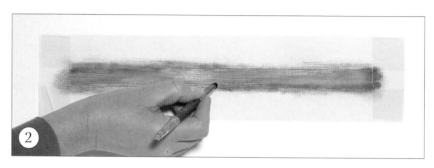

4. Mask the front edge of the shelf then create the shape for the top surface with masking tape. Repeat step 2 to paint the grain. Remove the tape.

5. Position the shelf bracket stencil under the shelf. Stencil this as shown in step 2. Repeat the stencil to complete the shelf then remove the tape.

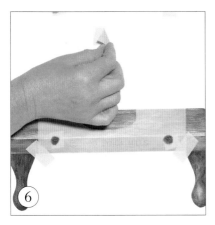

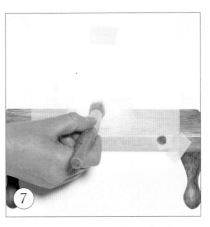

6. Position overlay 1 of the mug so that the bottom of the mug is 1cm (½in) above the top of the front edge of the shelf. Mark the registration dots. Mask out the knob at the top of the stencil.

7. Use a large brush and white paint to blank out the area of shelf showing through the stencil. Leave to dry.

8. Use a large brush and terracotta to apply a basecoat over the mug. Use a small brush and black paint to add shape and shade. Remove overlay 1.

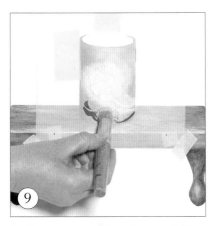

9. Position overlay 2, carefully matching the registration dots. Mask out the spout and the knob. Paint over the flower and leaf image with white paint.

10. Basecoat and shape the handle and the inside of the mug as shown in step 8. Stencil over the flower with yellow and green paint and use green for the leaf. Add shaping with black paint and a small stencil brush. Remove the stencil to reveal the completed mug.

11. To stencil the second mug, secure overlay 1 over the mug already worked, but slightly nearer to the front of the shelf. Mask out the knob and mark the registration dots.

12. Blank out the area that will be overpainted using white paint.

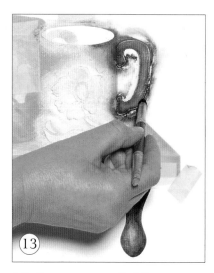

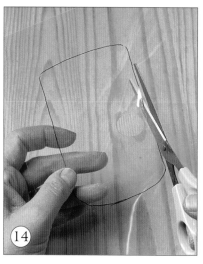

13. Repeat steps 8–10 to colour the second mug. Do not forget to blank out the part of the handle of the first mug showing through overlay 2. This process is stacking by overpainting.

14. To 'stack back' you need to produce a mask. To do this, trace the outline of the mug on to acetate (include the handle if necessary). Use sharp scissors to carefully cut out the image.

15. Tape the acetate mask into position over the first mug.

16. Place overlay 1 fractionally over and slightly higher than the masked mug. Mask out the knob. Blank out the shelf area to be overpainted, then use terracotta and black to colour the jug (see steps 7 and 8). Remove overlay 1.

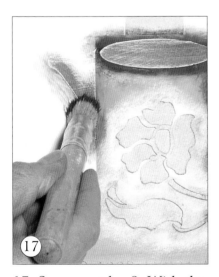

17. Secure overlay 2. With the knob masked, colour the rest of the jug, including the spout, using the techniques already shown.

18. Remove the overlay and the mask. Use terracotta and a touch of black with a small liner brush to colour the bridge on the spout of the jug. Add white highlights to the floral decoration and rims.

19. Mix a small amount of black paint with extender medium or water. Paint in the shadows around the jug, the mugs and the shelf using a large angled shader.

47

# PITFALLS TO AVOID

The two pictures on this page show some of the pitfalls to avoid when combining trompe l'oeil objects: confusing eye-level and stacking incorrectly. Another disaster waiting to happen is not being consistent with shadows. Shadowing is a valuable technique in trompe l'oeil work, providing wonderful opportunities to suggest volume, distance, texture, light quality and direction, as well as setting objects together in context. Make sure that you decide on the light direction before you start, and keep highlights, shading and shadowing compatible. It is also important to check that the sizes of the stencils you plan to combine are in proportion with each other, and of a similar style and design.

### MUGS ON SHELF

*A common mistake is to confuse eye-level in the same picture, and this painted image is a prime example. The left-hand mug is painted as if it were below eye-level, the right-hand one as if it were above eye-level and the shelf as if it were at eye level. The result is an incomprehensible, unrealistic picture!*

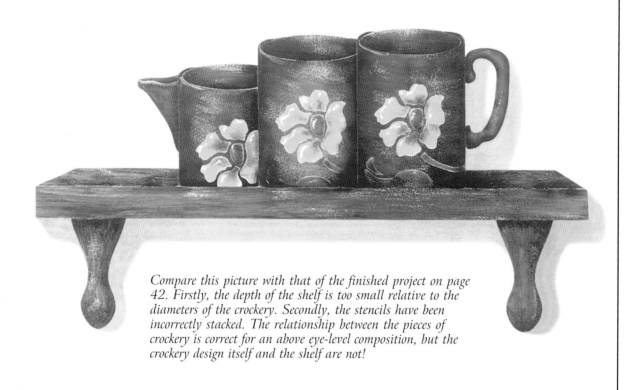

*Compare this picture with that of the finished project on page 42. Firstly, the depth of the shelf is too small relative to the diameters of the crockery. Secondly, the stencils have been incorrectly stacked. The relationship between the pieces of crockery is correct for an above eye-level composition, but the crockery design itself and the shelf are not!*

## WHITE CHINA

*You can stencil this impressive shelf using the same techniques and stencils as the project, but using alternative colours. If you enjoy practising your skills and playing with colours, you will develop a range of beautiful effects from the same stencil.*

# Umbrella plant

Freeform stencilling ~ Planning
Building a design ~ Environmenting

Freeform stencilling provides another exciting opportunity to
express your own individuality. Freeform features have many
advantages over static stencil designs. They are 'built' from a
variety of components, and their random placement can be used
to create an infinitely varied presentation. This provides the
freedom to customise size and shape, allowing for individual taste.

**YOU WILL NEED**

**Materials for stencil**: drafting
film, 90 x 60cm (36 x 24in),
permanent pen, masking tape,
glass cutting mat, scalpel, heat
pen or single hole punch

**Acrylic paint**: terracotta, light
brown, brown, mid-green, dark
green, black, white

**Stencil brushes**: 2 x small, 3 x
medium, 3 x large, 1 x liner
brush, 1 x large angled shader

**Other items**: palette, paper
towel, scrap paper, extender
medium

**PATTERN FOR THE
UMBRELLA PLANT**
*Enlarge each element on a
photocopier by 430% to
produce a plant with a pot
16.5cm (6½in) wide.*

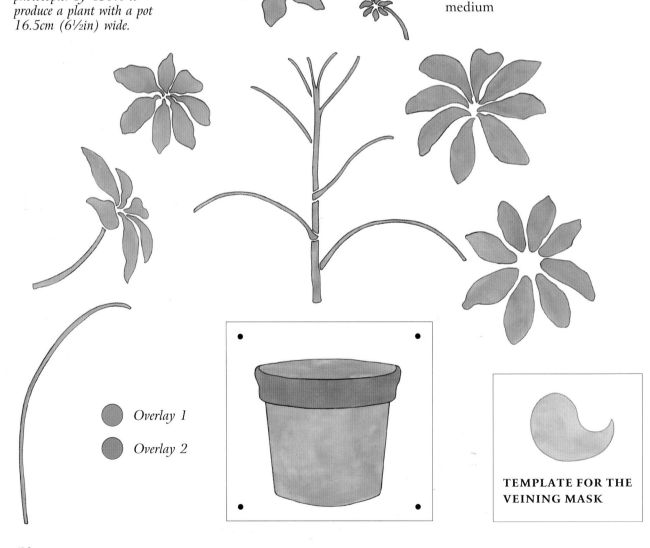

Overlay 1

Overlay 2

**TEMPLATE FOR THE
VEINING MASK**

**THE FINISHED
UMBRELLA PLANT**
*This is just one example of
the many possible layouts for
this plant. It can be 'built'
to any size and shape, by
using the component leaves.*

51

1. Lay out the leaves and consider positioning options on scrap paper first, to help identify the potential of the design.

2. Position and secure overlay 1 of the pot to your surface. Mark the registration dots. Basecoat with terracotta, using a large brush. Stipple with black and a medium brush to age and shape the pot. Highlight with light brown.

3. Remove overlay 1 and replace with overlay 2 of the pot. Line up the registration dots. Use the same colours as in step 2 to colour the rim of the pot. Remove the stencil.

4. Position the stalk stencil so that the end meets the lower rim of the pot. Blank out the area of pot showing through the stalk stencil, then lightly colour the stem using a large brush and mid-green. Add shape with dark green and a small brush. Remove the stencil.

**NOTE**
If you want to create a tall plant, you can extend the stem at this stage to the required height.

5. Position the small leaf stencil at the growth point at the top of the plant. Stencil with mid-green then shape with dark green. Remove the stencil.

6. Position the leaves that will appear at the back of the plant and colour them with mid-green. Add shape using a small brush loaded with dark green and black.

**NOTE**

It is best not to create veins on all the foreground leaves, as this can look contrived. Concentrate on one or two leaves in each cluster.

If you find the veining mask difficult to use, try using a liner brush.

7. Position a foreground leaf. Apply a dark green basecoat. Select part of the veining mask to match the shape of the leaf. Hold it in place and use mid-green to create a central vein. Add shape using black and a small brush. Repeat to create other foreground leaves. Remove all stencils.

8. Paint in the radial stems in the centre of each leaf cluster using a liner brush and mid-green.

9. Use a liner brush and mid-green to add or extend stalks.

**NOTE**

If you find it difficult to work freehand, use the stencil to add or extend stalks.

10. Add white highlights and touches of black to add definition to the leaves, stalks and pot.

54

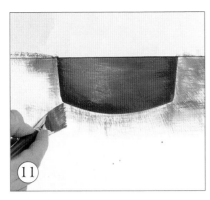

11. To provide a surface for the plant to sit on, use a straight edge or a piece of scrap paper to mask approximately three-quarters of the pot and all the plant. Mix a little brown paint with extender, load a large angled shader and stroke along the mask, then down around the pot.

**NOTE**

'Environmenting' or adding a surface will make a big difference to your trompe l'oeil images. Not only does it add realism and stop your objects from appearing to float, but it also gives the opportunity to shadow more effectively. Do not forget that shadows will alter when interrupted by another plane – so a shadow on a painted horizontal surface will abruptly change where it meets a vertical surface.

12. Mix black paint with extender and use this to add shadow. Remember to place the shadow away from the natural source of light in the room.

*Opposite*

**FREEFORM CLEMATIS DESIGN**

*This design is made up of several components which are repeated in different formats, thus convincing the eye of fresh, not tediously repeated, design. The stencils can be reversed (painted through the back), inverted (turned upside down) and used in differing orders and colours for maximum non-conformity. The flexibility of freeform enables you to easily customise a room by creating your own design that will fit perfectly.*

*This clematis was built from the elements shown below. With a little planning, mixing and matching, the components will produce an impressive plant of any shape or size.*

**COMPONENTS THAT MAKE UP THE
FREEFORM CLEMATIS DESIGN OPPOSITE**

# Marble fruit bowl

### Exploring texture ~ Working with extender

In this final project, textured surfaces are explored more fully. The stencil is a multi-overlay bridgeless design. The bowl lends itself particularly well to texture experimentation. In the pattern, I have included the fruit below the rim so you can practise stencilling glass (see page 63).

There are countless kinds of marble, granite and other types of stone, so there is plenty of opportunity to play with paint and develop skill. This project introduces the technique of marbling within a stencil, and this can be applied to the bowl shown here, or stencilled marble columns, pedestals or balusters. If a specialist faux artist were working a marble surface, glazes and many tools would be used to create the effect. With stencils, it is impossible to use glazes as they are too wet, and would immediately seep under the edges. So, I set out to create my own version of marbling that can be contained within a stencil . . .

**YOU WILL NEED**

**Materials for stencil**: 4 sheets of drafting film, 30 x 33cm (12 x 13in), permanent pen, masking tape, glass cutting mat, scalpel, heat pen or single hole punch

**Acrylic paint**: yellow, red, brown, grey, purple, green, burgundy, black, white

**Stencil brushes**: 3 x small, 6 x medium, 1 x large, 1 x liner brush and 1 x large angled shader

**Other items**: palette, paper towel, extender medium

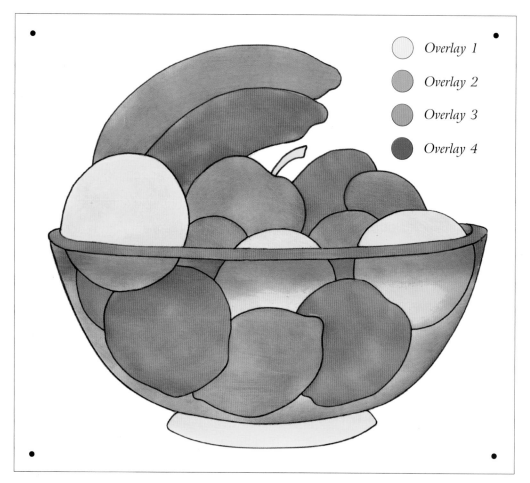

Overlay 1
Overlay 2
Overlay 3
Overlay 4

**PATTERN FOR THE FRUIT BOWL**
*Enlarge on a photocopier by 215% to create a finished design 25cm (10in) wide.*

1. Place overlay 1 on to your surface, secure it with masking tape and mark the registration dots. Mask the fruit below the bowl rim.

2. Use a medium brush and a mixture of yellow and red paint to stipple the oranges. Stipple the apple stalk using brown and a small brush. Add black shading to both.

3. Mix white with a little grey paint, then use a large brush to drag the base of the bowl. Use grey and a medium brush to shape, and black to shade.

4. Remove overlay 1.

5. Position overlay 2 and match the registration dots. Mask below the rim of the bowl, and paint the apple in green and red (see page 18). Mix black with purple then stencil the plum using a medium brush.

6. Remove overlay 2.

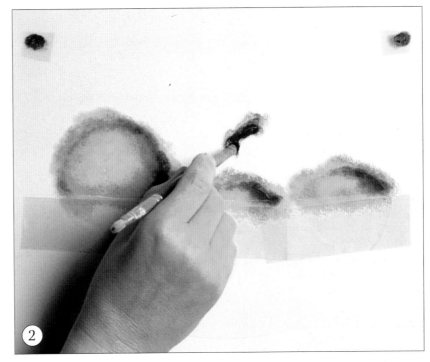

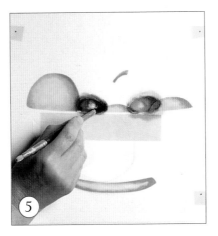

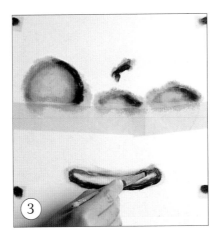

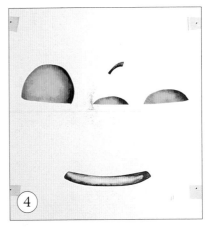

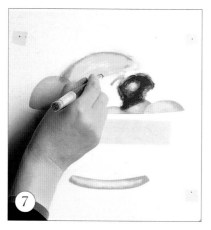

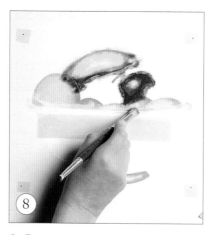

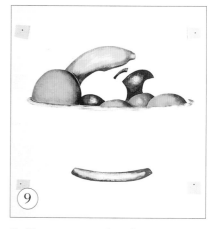

7. Position overlay 3, match the registration dots and mask below the rim. Stipple the plum as in step 5. Use a medium brush and yellow, brown and black to colour the banana.

8. Repeat step 3 to colour the rim of the bowl.

9. Remove overlay 3.

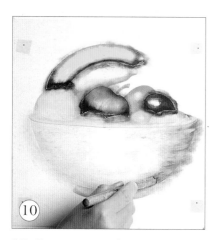

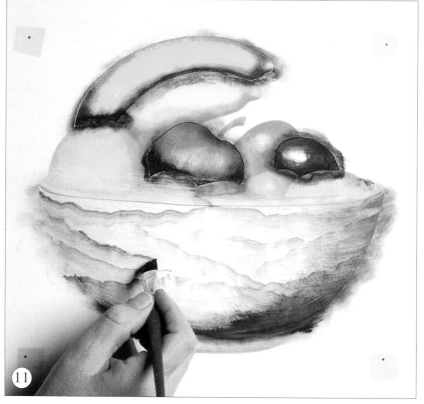

10. Position overlay 4, and match the registration dots. Use the same colours as before to paint in the apple, plum and banana. Drag the base of the bowl in off-white and shade to add shape.

11. Decant a puddle of extender on to your palette, then mix a little black paint into the medium to coat your angled shader. Dip just the tip of the brush into black paint then wipe it on the palette to mix slightly. Use slow, jagged, diagonal movements to add marble veins to the bowl. Allow the bristles to feather as you work, and try to follow the curve of the bowl.

60

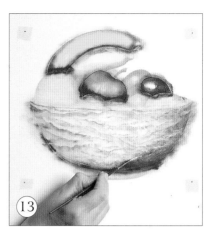

13. Use a liner brush to add white highlights and black shading to the veining.

12. Mix a little purple paint with extender. Use a small brush to stipple hints of colour over the bowl.

14. Remove overlay 4.

15. Remove the registration dots then mask off the top half of the bowl (see page 55). Mix a little burgundy paint with extender and use an angled shader to paint in an horizon and round the base of the bowl. Remove the mask, then use a little black mixed with extender to add shadow.

**THE FINISHED MARBLE FRUIT BOWL**

*Extender medium is a light gel which can be mixed with acrylic paint to 'open' it and to soften the colour intensity without losing the consistency of the paint. It enables you to achieve many subtle textures, including marble and glass.*

62

**GLASS FRUIT BOWL**

*The effect of glass is achieved by diluting grey with extender, and sweeping over the stencilled fruit. Curve your strokes to the shape of the bowl as you work. Use a dry brush to finish with sweeps of white – used sparingly, white is the effective route to shine!*

**WOODEN FRUIT BOWL**

*This bowl uses the same woodgraining technique as the shelf worked previously (see page 44). Mask the fruit below the rim, double-load a large brush with brown and black and then sweep with curved strokes echoing the shape of the bowl. Add shine with a dry white brush.*

# Index